CRACKING A NUT

Customer Service in the African Caribbean Business

Yvonne P Witter

Printed in the United Kingdom

ISBN 978-1-8384856-9-6

Published by BolaWit

Editorial Production: The Editor's Chair

Illustrations by Drew Sinclair
www.drewsinclair.wixsite.com/fineartist

ACKNOWLEDGEMENTS

Annmarie Dixon-Barrows, who was the best mentor ever. She opened doors for me and got me into two corporate leadership programs.

My son Duane Billy who inspires me to be a better person.

My late parents, Leonard and Iceyn Bailey from whom I learnt a punishing work ethic.

My editor, Denise Roberts, who steered me in the right direction.

Sister Kandake Makonnen, the herbalist, teacher and health advocate, who held my feet to the fire as we agreed a pact to simply meet and write together with writing goals and timelines.

RECOMMENDATIONS

Enjoyed reading this book. It is excellent the way the author weaves business preparation—or lack of—with featured small businesses and characters to focus on customer service, which is crucial to the success of any business. The book highlights the possible reasons why customer service among Black business seems to be such a poisoned chalice. Importantly, this is the first business-focused book I've read that can speak to potential entrepreneurs in the community conveyed in a way that they can easily relate to. Standard business templates and information has been a struggle for some in the past.

Starting a business is a serious decision when considering a new source of income after redundancy.

Money can be made if prepared to consistently work hard and put customer service and staff wellbeing at the core because without these there can be no viable long-term business.

Nadia Jones, Business Consultant, London

A great read, with a lot packed into what is a relatable story reminiscent of overheard conversations when I was growing up. I could see the film reel running and the characters in place, as the author highlighted and combined factual elements and storytelling set against a distinct African and West Indian scenery.

Jacqueline A Hinds MA (HRD) CEIC MCIPD
Founder & CEO of Society of Emotional Intelligence
International UK & Europe

Whether you are in business or just a casual observer, this book will give you ideas of what not to do. The author has captured the very essence of how the two experiences of good and bad service can co-exist and how many have come to expect the latter as the norm. No matter how experienced you are, this book reminds us of the importance of service, without which a great product will not make it in today's world.

The element of romance was a delightful surprise in the narrative, which made it easy to read. Totally needed for everyone in business or one to give to family and friends who run businesses. And if you are really bold, give it to a business owner with bad service—who knows, it might just be what they need to turn things around.

Lily Naadu Mensah, Brand Strategist

The message is clear: satisfied customers translate into a profitable business. Reading this book was a good reminder of how important customer service is. The book contains excellent real-world examples of customer service issues and encourages readers, especially business owners, to analyse their own customer service initiatives.

Tonya McNeal-Weary MBA AMC
Founder, IBS Global Consulting, Inc. & Think Global
Training Academy
Author, Women Going Global: Real-Life Stories of
Women Entrepreneurs Doing Business Across Borders

This is nostalgic and mirrors my experiences with some of these types of services. A great and informative capture of the changes we need to make within our business community.

Sherrine Barrowes, Psychotherapist, UK

I just got through reading *Cracking A Nut: Customer Service in the African Caribbean Business* by Yvonne Witter—it's an entrepreneur's guide to starting a business and a consumer's reminder of every bad business they've spent money in.

It's a short book of narrative and informative gold, combining learning, story and experience in an easy to follow and totally relatable story.

Yvonne is a natural storyteller and educator. She's chosen a simple and brilliantly effective way to package the learning material. I look forward to the audiobook version of this, and other titles in the series.

Eddie Hypolite, Australia
Director, Empowering Your Resilience PTY Ltd

Told through the lens of a young entrepreneur seeking guidance from his elders, this is a story that finally says what we've all been thinking—but with the added lessons on what to avoid and how. Without attacking, preaching, or pandering, *Cracking A Nut: Customer Service in the African Caribbean Business* explains, guides and connects the dots. A wonderful read and must-have in your entrepreneurial toolkit.

Lavinia Jones, Coach, UK

This well-written book takes us into a world we so very rarely hear about the black community, that of a loving community of relationships, where everyone supports each other. It is one where we learn from each other's mistakes and build on the foundation laid by previous generations. It's well-written, humorous, and kind, even as it calls out an area that needs to be developed in the community it's written for, namely, good customer service. All communities can learn from this book about the difference between servitude and service. As a psychotherapist who runs her own business, this is one of the requirements in being of service. The style is easily accessible and emotional coming from my now considered position as an elder.

So, thank you, Yvonne Witter, for writing this book. It feels and reads like a bestseller, and there is enough information there so that you can actually start a business. Well done.

Christa Welch, Psychotherapist, UK

My impression of this book is that it is an interesting way to talk about customer services in the Caribbean restaurant sector. So many of the images are accurate and a feature of many of these types of businesses, right down to the out-of-date flyers on the counter!

Karl Murray, Managing Director of FW Business Ltd

Contents

FOREWORD

Yvonne Witter, in *Cracking a Nut: Customer Service in the African Caribbean Business*, utilizes the mesmerizing impact of engaging storytelling to dialogue the need, principles and practice of stellar customer service.

This book showcases how the quality of both internal and external customer service can impact both the mindset of the organization's team and certainly the quality of the organization's overall service delivery to customers.

The power of customer service, both stellar and startling, is reflected in the attitudes and leadership behaviours of the delightful characters in this insightful customer service fable.

Yvonne also skillfully tackles the cloud that hovers over the African Caribbean Business too often, and that is service versus servitude, a mindset that can plague teams and businesses worldwide.

Infusing bits of history and culture, and clearly detailing the stark differences between the two, Witter offers invaluable insights which if acknowledged can serve to shift the mindsets and behaviours of those who serve others in any capacity.

Further, the author addresses the issues of wages, the training of team members, business ambience and branding, and striving to maintain a competitive edge through spectacular customer service and of course a value-added product.

Without question, this book is a must-read for every businessperson, and is a welcomed informational and training resource tool for practitioners and trainers!

Dr. Anita Davis-DeFoe USA
The John Maxwell Executive Director
CEO - Upshift Global and Collaborative Partner
with Healing Our Village, Inc. and HOV Build

Author, A Woman's Guide to Soulful Living: Seven Keys to Life and Work Success *and* Follow Her Lead: Leadership Lessons For Women As They Journey From the Backroom to the Boardroom, *Kwabena and the Baobab Tree*

INTRODUCTION

I am a generic business advisor, but, although not a specialism of mine, customer service has always intrigued me. Over the years, I have observed and researched how this practice of relating to customers is managed in different countries. I have come across many Black-owned businesses that offer excellent customer service at the point of service delivery and in after-sales. However, I have also seen how customer service in the African Caribbean business community is a topic of social conversation, frequently to the point of humour. Many of us can remember the 1993 BBC Real McCoy comedy sketch 'Misery West Indian Restaurant'.[1] This episode in the series

---

1   'Misery West Indian Restaurant' (1993). BBC The Real McCoy. Directed by Charlie Hanson. YouTube: https://youtu.be/ Ywv3kxCgtNk

encapsulated something many of us can relate to one way or another. My concern is that this disconnection with customers, although greatly improved since the nineties, persists in small samples of businesses in the community.

In 2012, I presented an academic paper titled *Service vs Servitude* at the Institute of Small Business and Entrepreneurship Annual Conference. At the time, I had ambitions to write a book about customer relationships, but I did not believe an academic book would have an impact on those small businesses operating in the marketplace who need to read it.

I was inspired by Simeon Quarrie, CEO of VIVIDA, to use storytelling as a tool to explain complex processes. I have used it in this book to incorporate the research and anecdotal evidence collected over the years. I considered this a helpful way to foreground some serious technical information. In writing this book, my aim has been to disrupt the current sentimentality and humour around the culture of poor service in certain service sectors. Many businesses do not thrive as much as they could because the customer service element of the business requires attention.

Blaming the public, competitors and staff when some business owners are lacking in management skills is not beneficial. In the past when only a few operators were offering culturally specific services, customers could suffer in silence or make a joke about our shared experiences as we consoled each other during the long waits or surly service. However, in what is now becoming an increasingly crowded marketplace with opportunities for online purchases too, the call to differentiate on every level is now high. It is important for us to realise that often, our core beliefs are not always based on fact, but more on perception.

I hope to have succeeded in creating a format that is accessible to most, a short story, which would encapsulate what most of us already know, whilst at the same time celebrating success and the opportunity for new ventures. My intention is to create a series of books on 'Cracking A Nut' so that *every* business can thrive. I hope that you find this first book in the series entertaining, informative and instructive.

Yvonne Witter MA FRSA CF

'Running a business is really hard work, but also quite rewarding on another level.'

CHAPTER ONE

The Barbershop

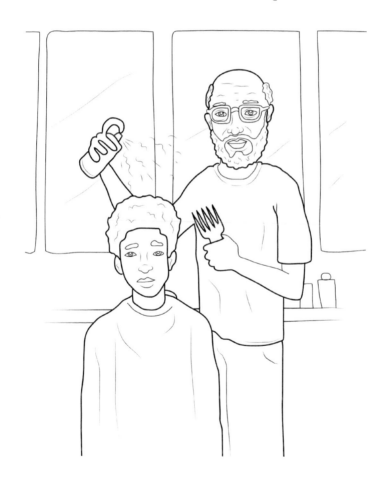

The sun bounced off the shiny shop front window as Paul pushed the brass handle to enter the barbershop.

'What's up, Cuz!' he greeted Winston and then fist pumped Ade who was sitting in the chair having his head shaved. The shop was unusually quiet this evening. Usually, on a Wednesday night, the local men would meet to offload, play a little domino and exchange information on where the best dance was happening, or the best place to buy the latest casual wear or gift ideas for the girlfriend or wife. Sometimes they discussed problems with the children or partner or whatever else was happening in their lives. It had been that way for years.

As Paul sunk into one of the barber chairs, memories came flooding back. His late father started bringing him to the shop before he could speak. Secretly, he used to call the place 'the manhood academy' because it was just like a university—whatever you wanted to find out, you could find it here. Even though it had been many years since Winston took it over from his pops, it hadn't lost that reputation. Paul knew the men could provide the guidance he needed to set up his new business.

His recent redundancy had come at just the right time as inheriting cash from his father. He had the time on his hands and as Bola, his girlfriend, was in a good job, they were quite comfortable now. Paul had always wanted to run his own business. Yes, he sighed inside; it was the right time.

'How tings going with the new shop, everything is everything?' Winston paused the buzz of the shaver to face Paul, his younger cousin, before returning to Ade's now bald scalp. 'Mek me know if you have any problems. Mi deh yah fi you, young soldier!'

Winston had been a big support ever since Paul's father had passed away.

'My last day of work was Friday,' Paul updated the men. He was looking forward to starting the business. It had always been a dream for his father too.

'I want to name it after my dad,' he told the men with a broad grin. 'Boyzie Bistro.' He made wide open arm gestures in the air as he explained his vision for shop signage in neon lights.

'It's not easy,' counselled Winston. 'Running a business is really hard work, but also quite rewarding on another level,' he added. 'Success comes from having a good relationship with customers, as well as the management of money and people.'[2]

Just then Colin emerged from the men's room to hear the last sentence and while giving a nod in Paul's direction, chimed in.

'Customers are so miserable they make me sick,' he said. 'They just make life so difficult for my business and dem rude!'

The men chuckled.

---

2   Wellington, P. (2010). *Effective Customer Care: Understand Needs, Improve Service, Build Relationships (Creating Success)*. S.L: Kogan Page.

'Every time you come in here, you bawl about how you vex with your customers,' Winston laughed. 'What business can run without customers?'

'I just wish somehow they didn't complain about everything.'

The men laughed again.

'Dream on my brother, dream on, because serving customers is what business is all about,' said Ade as he stood up and dusted off his jeans. 'If you don't have customers you don't have a business, and that goes for any kind of business.'

'I don't understand how you can say that customers are a problem when we have to have customers to sell to,' Winston added. 'Remember seh the customer brings in the money, so you can't forget that, big man.'

'Well, you just don't understand because you don't run a food business; it's different,' Colin protested.

Winston laughed again at his long-time friend. 'I've been running this barbershop for 20 years now and my customers are very important to me. It's a nut you need to learn to crack, my friend.'

But Colin simply kissed his teeth loudly, then turned to Paul.

'Young soldier, come up to my food shop on Wednesday around lunchtime. Mek me show you how dis ting work, never mind you cousin. Winston doesn't run a food business.'

'Go and see,' agreed Winston. 'It can't do you any harm, the more you learn the better.'

'Okay, I will see you next Wednesday then,' Paul agreed with a grin.

Paul had met Colin a few times as he was part of his late father's inner circle. He always thought of Colin as being impulsive, impatient, keen to cut corners and always in a hurry. He even spoke fast. Other than that, he was a nice enough man who now and again would slip him a tenner as a small child to 'go buy sweetie', as he would say.

'Gimmie two beef patty deh
Precious, quick time, mi park
bad'

CHAPTER TWO

Sell Me a Patty

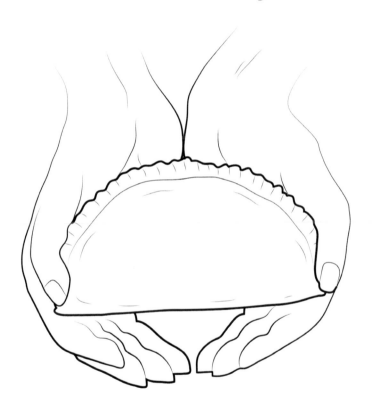

Paul found it difficult to park anywhere near Colin's shop. Red lines ran all along the main road and the resident parking signs on the side roads meant a fifteen-minute trek back to the shop. How did Colin accept deliveries? And what about customers who needed somewhere to park?

Outside, the shop signage had faded and condensation sat thick on the front window making it difficult to see inside. Paul pushed the door open. It triggered a loud chime mechanism, which startled him but did not seem to disturb the young lady sitting on a high stool behind the counter along the left side. Her head was down as she stared intently at her phone, her fingers dancing all over the screen. Colin was nowhere in sight.

As he stood waiting, Paul's eyes roamed around the small space. He mentally noted the overflowing bin and then examined the colourful array of flyers spread like confetti along the glass counter, advertising all white balls, a boat cruise to Amsterdam, carnival raves, bashment dances and double-glazing, some dating back some three years.

Beneath the counter in front of him sat six covered containers in steaming water. And on the wall beyond, the full Caribbean menu started with curried goat. Paul counted 16 items, which ended with 'steamed fish to order', but with no prices listed. He read the menu over and over, thinking about the complexity of preparing all those dishes.

'Hello Miss,' Paul called out, turning to the young lady.

She had not changed position since he walked in. Lifting her sweeping eyelashes, she shot him a cursory glance then looked back at her phone. He noticed her tightly coiffed hairdo which he thought made her look like she was destined for greater things than cook-shop server or whatever her job title was.

'Ah coming,' she said without looking up, 'one-minute deh.'

Then, before Paul could think to reply, she added, 'We only have curry goat and brown stew and jerk chicken today with plain rice or rice and peas, which one you want?' She looked up at him but did not move out of her seat.

'Oh, thank you, but I was looking for Colin, is he around?'

'Boss man gone to the shop, him say him soon come back,' she answered.

'Ok thanks, I will just wait.'

The young woman looked down and returned to tapping on her phone. Paul looked around. There were three round metal tables with plastic veneer and three chairs at each one. He placed his hand on one of the tables to steady himself as he took a seat and immediately wished he had not. Some kind of sticky substance had stuck to his hand. He pulled out a small packet of wet wipes and, after wiping his hands, ran it across the surface. All the other tables and chairs seem to carry the same dull sheen and the wall displayed a unique waterfall on canvass caused by the same condensation on the front window.

'Excuse me, Miss, do you know if he will be long?' Paul called to the lady.

'No, he can't be too much longer because him need the flour to make fried dumplings,' she replied without looking up.

Paul felt like he was disturbing the young lady each time he spoke to her so he put his earphones in and listened to some messages instead. The door opened, and he looked up expecting to see Colin, but a young man with swagger walked in wearing trainers that looked like they had just left the box. The young woman smiled and jumped to her feet.

'Gimmie two beef patty deh Precious, quick time, mi park bad,' shouted the man as he fixated his gaze through the haziness of the glass and onto his car parked outside on the red lines.

He rummaged in the pocket of his branded sweatpants and put some coins on the counter. Precious handed him a brown bag, and he turned and gave a cursory nod to Paul as he departed.

Paul was visualising his new shop when the door chimed again and a woman walked in. She wore beautiful locs that cascaded to her waist and looked like she might be on her lunch break from work. Paul thought she dressed like his girlfriend did: stack heeled ankle boots, black tights, black skirt, and a colourful blouse with a plain cardigan to match. She stood and studied the menu on the wall before asking if she could have the brown stew fish.

Precious remained seated as she told the woman the same as she had told Paul earlier. The woman asked if they had the Ital stew and Precious said no, only what she just said. Looking at the patties in the hot cupboard, the woman then asked if she could get a vegetable or saltfish patty.

'Dem finish, only beef and chicken left,' Precious told her.

On hearing this, the woman looked over at Paul and smiled awkwardly, then rolled her eyes to the heavens as she walked out. That loud chime and Precious kissing her teeth filled the musty air.

*   *   *

He leaned back in the chair
and surveyed the kitchen,
noticing that it looked equally
as chaotic as the shop area.

CHAPTER THREE

Is There a Problem with the Workers?

Moments later, the sound of the chime startled Paul this time. He opened his eyes to see Colin rushing in with a cigarette hanging out from the left side of his mouth and carrying a large plastic bag.

Pleased to see him, Paul rose to his feet.

'I wasn't expecting you so early, ah lunchtime now you know, and we busy.' He spoke quickly, cigarette ash dropping to his shirt.

'No problem,' said Paul. 'I am here to learn, so let me know if you need help with anything.'

'You can cook?' Colin shot him a look and they both laughed.

Colin invited Paul to join him in the kitchen at the back. He washed the rice, put it on to boil and then turned to his younger companion.

'I don't know what to do about this place,' he said.

'How do you mean?' Paul asked.

'Well, problems from start to finish, my youth. That's why I asked you to come so that you can see for yourself what you might be getting into. The customers have attitude when I tell them something on the menu isn't available. Like they want to make argument with me saying that if it's not available I shouldn't list it. It's just liberty; it's my shop so I can do what I want. They can buy what we have because I know my food tastes good.'

'Yes, everyone knows your food taste good, that you can cook good,' Paul agreed. 'I've seen you do plenty of weddings as a youth coming up.'

'I can't get good workers,' Colin continued, 'and that Precious only make a move when she's forced to.[3] All

---

3   Datta, K. & McIlwaine, C. et al. (2006). 'Work and survival strategies among low-paid migrants in London' [PDF file].

of them seem to be like that. No initiative. They come to work, but they're just not interested in working. What they want? More money? I'm building a house in the sun, so I can't afford to pay more than basic wages.'

He lowered his voice, as if just remembering that Precious was outside: 'Look at that one out there now—Precious. She's been here three months, and though I talk to her nothing change. She sits down on her phone from the time she walk in and she shows no interest. It's a favour I'm doing her, you know, helping her out, but no gratitude. I just don't understand these people.'

He paused for a moment to check the rice.

'Then to top it all, some red-eye grudgeful woman open a place right around the corner. They can't cook as good as me, yet the place ram out every day. People have no sense, seems like they will eat anything.'

London: Geography Department, Queen Mary University of London. Accessible at https://www.researchgate.net/publication/237756079_Work_and_survival_strategies_among_low-paid_migrants_in_London.

Colin shook his head as he added salt to the rice and stirred it.

'Oh yes, before me forget, this is the place where you can buy your goods wholesale at good price. Your seasonings and everything.' He handed Paul a piece of paper with a name and number.

'Thank you, that will be really useful,' Paul said. 'I was wondering though if you can provide training for your workers since you seem to be having a bit of trouble.'

'Training? What kind of training? I show them how to use the till and make change and they should know how to keep a place clean; they're women after all. Even me as a man know that tables need to wipe down and floor mop clean but unless I ask them directly, they don't do it. But when Friday come everybody hand stretch out. The last one complained that I didn't provide proper cleaning materials and gloves. Gloves you know?' Colin kissed his teeth long and hard.

'Maybe she wanted to protect her hands?' Paul said, half asking, half suggesting. 'Some of the cleaning chemicals can be abrasive to the skin and some people are allergic.'

'Well then, she should've walked with her marigolds innit?' Colin joked as he busied himself around the kitchen.

Paul laughed nervously. 'It's a difficult issue, I suppose.' He was starting to feel a sense of despair at Colin's attitude. He leaned back in the chair and surveyed the kitchen, noticing that it looked equally as chaotic as the shop area. Colin interrupted his thoughts.

'You know seh if I don't stay open well into the night, I can't make any money?' Colin asked. 'So, when *sheeee* across the road closes, that is when *I* get a little chance. We used to be the only shop for miles selling the best Caribbean food. This place was full from breakfast till after lunch and we could close at 6pm. Now every ting change. My wife blames me, says that I gamble too much, but it's not that. People don't support like they used to do. Everyone seems to like shiny new tings. Where's the loyalty, eh?'

*   *   *

Paul was intrigued.
'What does that mean, service versus servitude?'

CHAPTER FOUR

Service or Servitude?

The barbershop had a familiar smell of cologne and shaving creams mixed, which created a unique aroma of sandalwood, patchouli, eucalyptus, and lavender. There were ornate framed pictures of famous sportsmen, musicians and visiting American and Caribbean celebrities posing with Winston. They had all benefitted from Winston's dexterity with shavers and their happy, smiling faces adorned the walls. These photographs created a gallery alongside group photos of staff on special occasions, like shop refits or seasonal gatherings. Newspaper and magazine spreads had pride of place in custom-built frames.

The sumptuous black leather chairs that reclined and spun were comfy places that no customer wanted to rise out of when the time came. Often Winston could be heard jokingly telling a customer, 'You can get up now, we're all done you know.'

A whiff of coffee aroma drifted from the corner of the shop where customers could select from an array of hot beverages. In the cupboard below was the serious stuff, courtesy of J Wray & Nephew. This came out after hours or on special occasions, alongside red or white rum with a chaser to celebrate a birth, or a birthday, or to commiserate a passing.

On many occasions people would simply pop in to leave a 'gift'. Sometimes a customer would go on holiday and bring back a bottle of fine rum, or a parcel of mangos from the Caribbean. People who started their careers in the shop would stop by to pay homage, sometimes with a visiting family member or friend.

Things had gone well for Winston, so much so that he was able to expand the shop into the small unit next door. The new space offered beauty therapies and natural hair grooming. Many men would wear locs but also want a face shave and to have their edges tidied up, so it offered convenience. Beverly did the facial massage and various beauty therapies, and Carol was the loctitian. Although it was a barbershop, it provided so much more than this as a community hub.

Winston seemed to have a clear vision of what he wanted for his customers and so Paul could not wait to relay what he had witnessed to get some feedback.

'That sounds like a baptism of fire,' said Winston after Paul had finished telling him about his visit. Both men laughed.

'I didn't know what to expect but when I popped into the new shop around the corner to see what Colin was talking about, I found a bright clean sparkling place, a bit like this, Cuz. People ordered their food and were queuing up to be served. The staff were chatty and welcoming and friendly.[4] The food looked freshly cooked, well-presented and piping hot. It was all laid out in the containers so people could see, and everything on the menu was on sale. A mix of vegetarian and fish dishes too. One person was

---

4   American Dental Association. (2007). 'The Power of Customer Service: How to Create Happy Satisfied Customers' [PDF file]. Chicago: American Dental Association. Accessible at http://harleyhussain.xyz/download/zir6zp8ueEQC-the-power-of-customer-service-how-to-create-happy-satisfied-patients.

clearing and wiping tables meanwhile people were getting seated.

'It's a small café, but it's so nice and clean that people seemed to want to stay and eat too. There was some pleasant music playing extremely low in the background creating a nice ambience. The place was well lit and bright, almost like sunshine,' he chuckled.

'One problem we have is that sometimes we start a business and get too big for our own boots,' Winston said. 'We forget that others are coming up with similar ideas and that we need to stay ahead of the curve. If we don't stay ahead, we'll end up sliding down on that curve.

'Some people pay low wages because they can, especially if papers aren't sorted and workers are desperate. To top it all we have great expectations of those that we employ on minimum wages. Cuz, there's a fine line between service versus servitude.'

Paul was intrigued. 'What does that mean, service versus servitude?'

'Servitude's driven by reward; the goal of a person in servitude is to earn the reward,' Winston began.

He had adopted the 'scholarly' tone he reserved for serious matters and Paul knew he was in for some deep learning.

'On the other hand,' Winston continued, 'when providing a service, the biggest satisfaction is to see the recipient satisfied. There's an inner feeling of self-esteem and fulfilment by the service provider. Servitude's associated with slavery and inhuman acts, which people with a history of enslavement often want to dissociate themselves from. So, there might be some unconscious confusion, a mix-up.'

'Wow, you really think that?' Paul sat in his chair spinning halfmoon, back and forth, watching the steam on his waiting mug of hot chocolate.

'Is not me thinking that,' said Winston switching vernaculars momentarily, 'there's research to back it up. Service is associated with creating a good rapport with the person being served.[5] In a situation of servitude, a master is the boss and the servant should

---

5   Pietro, S. D., 2010. 'Service V Servitude'. Accessed on 8th July 2013 at http://servingmatters.blogspot.com/2010/04/service-v-servitude.html

satisfy that master by doing what he's asked otherwise he won't be rewarded.'

Winston was using a chamois to clean the workstation mirrors, moving from one area to the next, each time leaving the glass sparkling like diamonds.

'Yes!' said Colin. 'That's exactly how it seemed.' He jumped out of his chair and waved his arms around as he recalled his experience in Colin's shop. 'It's like he just wants to boss people around and not train them properly. He didn't even greet her when he walked into the shop, and he kept talking bad about her. I'm sure she could hear him, but he didn't seem to care, even told me that he was doing his workers a favour by providing employment at low wages.'

'Rhatid!' Winston stopped to lean against a counter, crossing one leg over the other. He shook his head. 'Service focuses on ensuring the person receiving the service is satisfied and feels appreciated, not the other way around,'[6] he said. 'The customer's kept at the

---

6   American Dental Association. (2007). 'The Power of Customer Service: How to Create Happy Satisfied Customers' [PDF file]. Chicago: American Dental Association. Accessible at http://

heart whenever delivering the service. But servitude focuses on adhering to the rules of the master to ensure they're followed to the letter. So, good service comes from focusing fully on a customer, rather than on the master's reaction.'

'Well, there's no interest in customers there, although one man came in who seemed to be a friend or something because the girl, Precious, she jumped to her feet to tend to him as he walked in. That was the only time I saw any smile or warmth in the place.'

Winston sighed. 'Well, the relationship between the master and servant in servitude is a dull one, with both parties completely at different levels of interaction,' he said. 'The servant's destined to be the loser in these interactions and isn't motivated to do a good job. This could explain the general experience of poor service in small high street shops where staff are apathetic, and in low paid positions in retail and catering.'[7]

---

harleyhussain.xyz/download/zir6zp8ueEQC-the-power-of-customer-service-how-to-create-happy-satisfied-patients

7   Wright, T. & Pollert, A. (2006). 'The Experience of Ethnic Minority Workers in the Hotel and Catering Industry: Routes to Support and Advice on Workplace Problems'. London: Research Institute, London Metropolitan University. Accessible

Paul was now sitting back on his chair. He took a sip of his hot chocolate and then licked his lips. 'Okay,' he said decisively, 'fair enough, but if I own the business, as the owner-manager, surely it's in my interest to keep everything going good so I can make money and be successful. I'm now wondering if there's an unconscious fear in the African Caribbean community of us performing as "slaves" by providing a service?'[8]

at https://www.researchgate.net/publication/241516376_The_Experience_of_Ethnic_Minority_Workers_in_the_Hotel_and_Catering_Industry_Routes_to_Support_and_Advice_on_Workplace_Problems

8   Misery West Indian Restaurant (1993). [Film] Directed by Charlie Hanson. UK: BBC *The Real McCoy*.

His brow knotted, and his voice became louder as he paced back and forth.

CHAPTER FIVE

Who Can I Trust?

'**M**aybe there's a level of inherent mistrust,' Winston agreed as he sat down in one of the barber chairs and began to work on a smudge he had missed on the mirror. 'Marcus Garvey said if people had trusted him, he would have been able to liberate many.[9] Maybe this mistrust creates tension, or friction, or bad mind between the customer and the business owner and their low-paid workers. I've seen customers walk into places and talk down to the staff rudely, which is totally unacceptable, and I always wondered what that's all about.[10] When it happens here, I stomp it out immediately. Notice the signs all around the shop?'

9   Garvey, M. (1988). Marcus Garvey Life Lessons. S. L: University of California Press.

10   Dubois, W. (1903). The Souls of Black Folk. Chicago: A.C. McClurg & Co.

He pointed to the walls. 'In my place respect is a two-way street!'

Paul jumped out of his chair and paced the floor.

'All I know is that with my business I want to ensure business growth and sustainability. I want to create a close and productive relationship between my customers and myself and my workers. I want my customers to leave my place feeling so satisfied that they tell other people and I get repeat customers. That's what I'm going to be working towards.'[11]

His brow knotted, and his voice became louder as he paced back and forth.

'I want loyalty from my customers,' Paul continued, 'and I know I'll have to earn that because they always have the choice to shop somewhere else. I can't forget the look on that woman's face when they had nothing on the menu she could eat.' He shook his head and looked down at the floor.

---

11   Wellington, P. (2010). *Effective Customer Care: Understand Needs, Improve Service, Build Relationships (Creating Success).* S.L: Kogan

'I don't want anyone working for me to feel under pressure and in fear, and only perform because I'm standing over them barking at them, no sah!'[12]

He shook his head again but this time more vigorously.

'I want my workers to feel happy to provide a service and I won't stop looking until I find the right staff because it's important to me that people represent me well whether or not I'm in the shop.' He banged his fist on the workstation nearest to him.

'Calm down, son, all is well,' Winston chuckled, noticing the young man's anxiety, passion and determination. 'You sound smart, the way you put it. Those are good ambitions. You remind me of your old man.'

He reflected for a moment before continuing with his insights.

---

12   Wright, T. & Pollert, A. (2006). 'The Experience of Ethnic Minority Workers in the Hotel and Catering Industry: Routes to Support and Advice on Workplace Problems'. London: Research Institute, London

'You know that servitude was prevalent during colonialism and many Caribbean and African nations have a rich colonial history, right? Well, during that period, a system of servitude was used to exercise power over others. But the current customer service model of operating that you see in the big stores nowadays is modern and relatively new, and it's a method of serving people. So, it's different. Servitude existed when it was believed that some people were superior and others were inferior, but in advanced nations where equality's included in statutes, service has replaced servitude and human dignity is mostly being upheld.'[13]

'Ooohhh,' Paul said as it all continued to sink in. He was leaning against the wall, arms folded across his chest and nodding his head like the Churchill dog in the TV advert, only slower. 'So it's like a cultural thing? A throwback from a bygone era? That would explain a lot, because many people have an old-fashioned approach to life, or they may come here from a different country and bring that attitude with

---

13   Rich, J. & Orr, L. (2012). Enhanced Customer Satisfaction. One Zero Seven.

them.' He shook his head side to side. 'That's deep, Cuz.'

'Remember though that servitude and service are two very distinct terms.' Winston wagged his index finger to reinforce his point. 'They shouldn't be used interchangeably, and the practices shouldn't be confused, because while service is seen as a noble act by society and many religions, servitude is detested by all as it's seen as modern-day slavery.'[14]

'Cuz, you're a walking Wikipedia.' Paul shook his head in awe.

'No, is not dat,' said Winston, returning to his street lingo. 'We never stop learning if we're open to it. Life's a journey, not a destination, so said Ralph Waldo Emerson. Cuz, always keep an open mind and treat people as you yourself would like to be treated, as cleanliness is next to godliness.'

---

14 Anti-Slavery International. (2013). Accessed on 8th July 2013 at http://www.antislavery.org/english/slavery_today/what_is_modern_slavery.aspx

He gave the mirror a final rub as both men laughed. Then Winston stood up, walked over to his cousin and they embraced each other.

*   *   *

'Do you remember that BBC comedy, *The Real McCoy*? That sketch they did called "Misery West Indian Restaurant"?'

CHAPTER SIX

Let's Get Started

Paul made great strides with his business after what he learned from his cousin. He was introduced to a business officer, someone his girlfriend found via a contact in the business and economy department at the local government offices where she worked. He was surprised to find out how helpful and supportive people were in providing information about business registration, premises licensing, banking and all the regulations regarding food handling and employment rights.

Paul purchased a small cabinet to keep his papers and documents as he recalled the story of Leroy, a local plumber who married a young woman from abroad. All was going reasonably well, but he had not put his papers away securely and the baby one day poured drinks and food all over his files. The joke was that the two-year-old was doing paper mâché. His wife was on the phone at the time on a long-distance phone call to her friend back home.

The destruction of his paperwork nearly ruined his business because he struggled to complete his accounts and file his tax returns as nearly a year's worth of invoices and purchase receipts were destroyed. This was before people started doing everything online and Leroy was just learning how to use the computer for his business.

Although Paul had heard the story in the context of having a certain kind of wife from overseas, the situation regarding the business stuck with him. He made an appointment to meet up with a business advisor who would support him to write his business plan. This included budgeting, cash flow forecasting[15] and learning how to use online accounting software; all this information was invaluable to him since running a business was a new journey.[16]

He attended half-day seminars on marketing management and communications for small

---

15   https://www.startuploans.co.uk/cash-flow-forecast-template/
16   https://www.gov.uk/write-business-plan

businesses, building customer relationships, social media marketing, hiring staff, calculating tax and national insurance and an understanding of basic employment law. Paul's girlfriend Bola even attended some seminars with him and when they got home, they discussed what they had learnt and worked on the business plan.

This recent interest of Paul's had brought them closer together. He was devastated after his father's passing, and then there was his redundancy three months ago. Bola and Paul had always been able to have difficult conversations but at first she had a real fear he might feel pushed over the edge, even though he never did like that job much, often feeling he had been passed over for promotion too many times. But it was a lot to have happened in the space of a year. She felt challenged in finding the courage to speak to Paul about the matter but knew she had to share her concerns over his mental health. Thankfully, it worked out that this opportunity for timeout and reflection gave him a new lease of life and set him on a fresh path.

Now here they were working together to bring Paul's vision to life. They both qualified as food handlers, and Paul was excited that Bola was showing so much interest in the business; he secretly hoped that she might join him full-time as a business partner.

Bola had done a lot of research online to find reclaimed kitchen equipment at reasonable prices. Sometimes they stayed up well into the night designing the shop and thinking about the colour scheme and layout. They visited many cafes, bistros and restaurants to get ideas. The council was also quite helpful for providing information on suitable locations, and common sense regarding opening times, parking spaces, foot-fall [the volume of passers-by each day] and security had an influence on the location they would choose.

One night, Bola and Paul were wrapping up another evening of discussing the business and adding to the business plan. They did not need the business plan to raise finances but working through the template with the business advisor guiding them provided them with much clarity regarding all aspects of the business.

'Winston told me loads of things I didn't learn at any of the business training,' he told Bola.

'Really? Like what?'

'All I know is that we really can't fall into the same trap many others do by treating our staff poorly or not serving customers well.'

Bola laughed knowingly.

'Hmmm, soon as you mention cookshop is pure jokes, innit? Wait! Do you remember that BBC comedy, *The Real McCoy?* That sketch they did called "Misery West Indian Restaurant"? I mean, that made it to the BBC yah know! I was only small at the time. Someone mentioned it at work last week. Did you know that all episodes are available on YouTube?'

'Let's find it online,' Paul said excitedly.

As the comedy sketch played out, both Bola and Paul were in stitches. They laughed until they had tears in their eyes, shouting over each other every time they recognised a particular familiar experience.

'The other challenge I suppose
is that low-paid workers can't
be expected to work beyond
their pay grade.'

CHAPTER SEVEN

Being of Service

The following day, Bola and Paul woke up in high spirits. They had appointments to visit four potential locations for the new African Caribbean bistro. They joked, teased, and played around as they prepared to leave.

*   *   *

It was a long day for them, dodging raindrops, parking on meters and occasionally finding a nearby car park. They visited two places that were closed down cafes and two other buildings that would need to be fitted out for purpose and licensed to trade as a food preparation and sales business. They arrived home tired but stimulated by what they had seen. The two looked through the many pictures they had taken and made notes.

As the evening grew late, they ordered dinner in from their favourite Italian restaurant. While relaxing and eating, Paul explained what he understood from his conversations with Winston about service versus servitude. Bola was quite fascinated by this new information, and immediately it resonated with her too.

'But poor customer service is not a feature of most of the small, owner-managed restaurants and shops that exist,' she noted. 'Is that because of the provision of customer service training or a different attitude to the customer? Do people from other groups have no unconscious fear of performing the role of a servant or slave in providing a service to others?'

'Have you noticed that most of those small businesses are staffed by men?' Paul asked. 'I wonder if it would be different if many more women were customer-facing too.[17] I'm not sure how it is that many small owner-managed businesses do an okay job at being friendly and polite to customers—even though you can see it's not always genuine because of the coldness in their eyes. At least they make an effort to serve.'

---

17 Bales, K. & Robbins, P. T. (2001). 'No One Shall Be Held in Slavery or Servitude: A critical analysis of international slavery conventions'. Human Rights Review, 2(2), pp. 18-45.

He sighed and leaned back in his chair.

'Customer service is a whole industry in and of itself, and the small business owner can't really afford all that's involved. Also, that level of customer service intervention is not necessary in the same way it would be in a massive department store, for example, with thousands of products and hundreds of customers.'

Bola nodded thoughtfully. 'The other challenge I suppose is that low-paid workers can't be expected to work beyond their pay grade,'[18] she said.

'So,' Paul said mischievously. 'How do we make sure we don't become another Misery cafe?'

They both burst out laughing.

'Poor working conditions might explain the resentment and dissatisfaction of workers in the catering industry in developed nations,' Bola said returning to making her point. 'However, back in

---

18 Wright, T. & Pollert, A. (2006). 'The Experience of Ethnic Minority Workers in the Hotel and Catering Industry: Routes to Support and Advice on Workplace Problems'. London: Research Institute, London

African countries and in the Caribbean, for example, where front line government officers are providing a public service, how do we explain the experiences of poor customer service in that context? Is that then related to a cash-strapped service sector that does not have the infrastructure or resources to implement and maintain a customer service ethos?'

'Could be the case,' said Paul. 'But service is about giving a part of you to help another. That's it. It comes from the *intent* to help another. Servitude comes when you help with the intent of return. Servitude is inwardly focused on return. In slavery, the internal return is self-preservation; you did what you had to do to stay alive or safe. Do as your owner demands or face dire consequences. Service however comes from wanting to serve the recipient, not from wanting to please the boss.'

'Paul?' Now it was Bola who sounded mischievous.

'Yes?' Paul answered.

'Would you like some service?'

They both giggled.

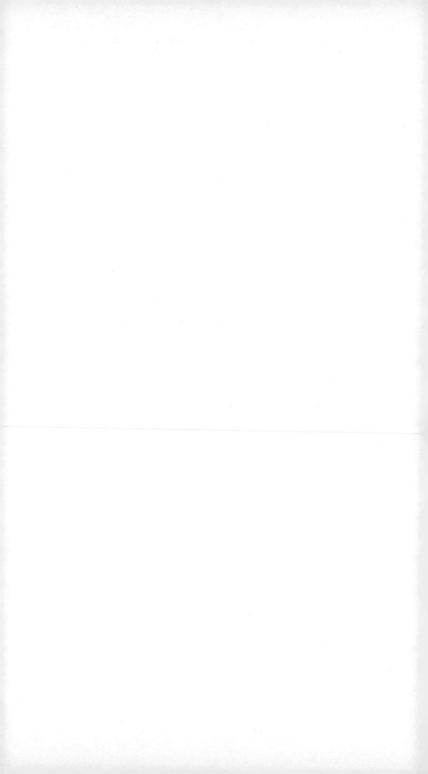

Opening night was buzzing;
the bubbly was flowing, and
the food looked delicious.

CHAPTER EIGHT

Time to Celebrate

Winston rarely got the opportunity to enjoy evenings out with Gloria because he was often too tired after closing the barbershop. Gone were the days when he would rush home, have a quick shower and then breeze out again. Gloria, too, was often fawning over her young grandchildren in the evenings. Tonight was special; they had chosen their outfits carefully, Gloria had taken the day off from her senior teaching position and Winston had not gone into the barbershop. As they linked arms and walked down the brightly lit street, they could hear the gentle hum of music. Then they saw the big unmistakable neon sign: 'BOYZY BISTRO'. Written beneath in large letters was 'African Caribbean Cuisine'.

Winston had seen pictures of the place and visited when the contracts were being signed. He had helped with licensing the premises with the local government department. Yet, he was blown away by the attention to detail in every aspect of the décor and fittings. Bola and Paul had roped in friends and family to help with the painting, murals, fixtures and fittings. Even Colin had assisted with getting some nearly-new reclaimed kitchen equipment.

Opening night was buzzing; the bubbly was flowing, and the food looked and smelt delicious. There was a lovely cake set aside with the shop's neon sign laser imaged on the top. The atmosphere was warm and friendly, and Paul and Bola were soon swallowed up by the small crowd of familiar faces from far and wide, hugging and greeting each other.

'May I have your attention, please? Hello! Hello!' Paul shouted above the din.

Finally, there was a hush, and the DJ stopped the music. Everyone shouted 'speech, speech' at which Paul blushed. There was no turning back now, all eyes were on him.

'Bola, Bola, come here, please. I need you by my side.'

Everyone cooed and awed at the young couple, as Bola made her way through the parting crowd.

'May I take this opportunity to thank you all for coming out on a Wednesday evening to celebrate with us the opening of this café in memory of my father, who you all know as Boyzy. Every single person in here tonight has given me support and words of encouragement or helped in some way to make this dream of mine a reality.'

He cleared his throat as he pulled Bola closer to him.

'Cuz Winston opened my eyes to a few new ideas about the importance of the customer to a business, and I want to thank him from the bottom of my heart because I learnt so much, truss me.'

Paul pulled out a piece of paper from his pocket.

'Boyzy Bistro is committed to serving customers with a smile. We intend to always keep our establishment clean and presentable and treat all staff and customers with respect. We can't pay the highest wages, but we will pay a fair living wage in line with government recommendations. We believe that kindness and being polite costs nothing, so we can do that 24/7 to keep everyone happy. If you look over there on your right, you will see our customer service standards which set out our commitment to being of service to our customers. So again, I want to thank you all for coming.'

Paul put the paper back into his pocket and everyone applauded and started talking again.

He cleared his throat.

'Oh, just one more thing,' he reached into his breast pocket and removed a small box. His voice quivered slightly as he spoke again.

'Bola,' he said turning to look into her eyes. 'I would like to ask for your hand in marriage.'

Bola laughed and hugged him and then they kissed in a long embrace.

Immediately, the DJ turned to his deck and spun Tarrus Riley, 'She's Royal',[19] and the room erupted as

---

19   Tarrus Riley She's Royal https://youtu.be/qGuLqe-NMKg

everyone sang to the lyrics and Paul slipped the ring on Bola's finger.

'Cut the cake!' Winston shouted.

Bola and Paul cut the cake together and everyone laughed and applauded, saying that it was a good rehearsal for the wedding.

They served the cake on small plates with a fork and napkin, and the music went up a notch as the revellers continued to celebrate and cheer on the new business and the newly engaged couple.

BoyZy Bistro
Customer Service Charter

We Aim To

Source quality fresh produce and groceries from reliable suppliers.

Ensure that our staff are knowledgeable and fully trained.

Positively encourage and will act swiftly on customer feedback.

Comply fully with all relevant legislation.

Open the shop on time and ensure that it is clean.

Exceed customer expectations in all that we do.

Our Staff

Will be approachable, and friendly.

Will treat all customers with patience, respect, and courtesy.

Will respond to any customer complaints in a professional and timely manner.

Will deliver a positive customer experience for all who enter our shop.

Promise to be forward-thinking in anticipating customer needs.

Customers

We expect customers to treat our staff with respect and courtesy.

To be considerate to other customers.

To respect the physical space of the shop and use the bins provided.

Get in Touch

Yvonne Witter is available for speaking engagements and book signings.

Email: hello@crackinganut.com
Visit: www.crackinganut.com

BIBLIOGRAPHY

American Dental Association. (2007). 'The Power of Customer Service: How to Create Happy Satisfied Customers' [PDF file]. Chicago: American Dental Association. Accessible at http://harleyhussain.xyz/download/zir6zp8ueEQC-the-power-of-customer-service-how-to-create-happy-satisfied-patients

Anti-Slavery International. (2013). Accessed on 8th July 2013 at http://www.antislavery.org/english/slavery_today/what_is_modern_slavery.aspx

Bales, K. & Robbins, P. T. (2001). 'No One Shall Be Held in Slavery or Servitude: A critical analysis of international slavery conventions'. *Human Rights Review*, 2(2), pp. 18-45.

Datta, K. & McIlwaine, C. et al. (2006). 'Work and survival strategies among low-paid migrants in London' [PDF file]. London: Geography Department, Queen Mary University of London. Accessible at https://www.researchgate.net/publication/237756079_Work_and_survival_strategies_among_low-paid_migrants_in_London.

Dubois, W. (1903). *The Souls of Black Folk.* Chicago: A.C. McClurg & Co.

Garvey, M. (1988). *Marcus Garvey Life Lessons.* S. L: University of California Press.

King, M. L. (2001). *The Autobiography of Martin Luther King.* S. L: Grand Central Publishing.

'Misery West Indian Restaurant' (1993). [Film] Directed by Charlie Hanson. UK: BBC *The Real McCoy.*

Pietro, S. D., 2010. 'Service V Servitude'. Accessed on 8th July 2013 at http://servingmatters.blogspot.com/2010/04/service-v-servitude.html

Rich, J. & Orr, L. (2012). *Enhanced Customer Satisfaction*. One Zero Seven.

Wright, T. & Pollert, A. (2006). 'The Experience of Ethnic Minority Workers in the Hotel and Catering Industry: Routes to Support and Advice on Workplace Problems'. London: Research Institute, London Metropolitan University. Accessible at https://www.researchgate.net/publication/241516376_The_Experience_of_Ethnic_Minority_Workers_in_the_Hotel_and_Catering_Industry_Routes_to_Support_and_Advice_on_Workplace_Problems

Wellington, P. (2010). *Effective Customer Care: Understand Needs, Improve Service, Build Relationships (Creating Success)*. S.L: Kogan Page.

Witter, Y. P. (2013). '"Service" or "Servitude"'. Accessed on 8th July 2013 at http://stjohnssalisbury.org/index_htm_files/service-vs-servitide.pdf

ABOUT THE AUTHOR

Yvonne Witter entered the world of enterprise working part time as a Business Start-Up Skills Trainer, writing and delivering short courses in a South London Community College, whilst holding down a full-time job as a Centre Manager elsewhere. In 2003, she achieved the gold standard in business advisor training back then when she became accredited by the Small Firms Enterprise Development Initiative (SFEDI). That year, Yvonne launched Ampod Limited and went on to procure government contracts to deliver business coaching, training, advice and mentoring with the support of a team of professionals. In 2012, she set up Yvonnepwitter Consulting to provide more tailored support to small business owners and social entrepreneurs. Although she marks these as the start of her journey, her passion for business was sown decades earlier as a child as she helped out in her parents' small business. These early seeds charted her course to qualify in Business Studies and Communications.

Over her career, Yvonne has worked holistically with organisations, small businesses, individuals, sole traders, limited companies, social enterprises and NGOs in the United Kingdom, Europe, Africa, the Caribbean and the Far East. She has amassed a wealth of experience in all aspects of business start-up, capacity building, growth and sustainability across various business cultural landscapes.

Today, Yvonne continues to provide services to empower and inspire people to create a life by design. Her mission is to enable people to expand and innovate in business by helping them to manifest their dreams into reality.